The Woman at the Well

Seen, Known, & Transformed

A 10-day Devotional Journey Through John 4

Nakita T. Bell

This book is intended for inspirational and devotional purposes only. It is designed to encourage personal reflection, spiritual growth, and thoughtful examination of patterns and experiences. It is not intended to provide medical, psychological, legal, financial, or other professional advice. Readers are encouraged to seek appropriate professional guidance where needed. The author and publisher disclaim any liability arising directly or indirectly from the use or application of the contents of this book.

The Woman at the Well - Seen, Known, & Transformed

A 10-Day Devotional Journey Through John 4

ISBN: 978-0-9959307-2-8 (Paperback)

Dedicated to the Loving Memory of:

Ruth Theodora Clarke, my dearest Grandma

&

William Campbell McLaren (Billy), my devoted Stepdad

Thank you for choosing to spend the next ten days with this devotional book. As you move through these pages, my prayer is that you encounter God in a way that feels personal and timely.

Each chapter invites you to draw from Scripture, not just to gain understanding, but to allow the Word to speak into your life. Before beginning each day's reading, take time to sit with the passage itself, letting the words settle before continuing into the devotional.

This devotional was written to help you see how the truth of God's Word still applies today and how it continues to shape and transform us from the inside out.

My hope is that as you read, something begins to stir within you, that God's love becomes more than a concept, and that you find yourself taking steps toward the life He has called you to.

With love,

Nakita

Overview of John 4

This account takes place in a town called Sychar, located in the region of Samaria, where Jesus stopped while traveling from Judea to Galilee. As news of His growing ministry spread, people were drawn to His teachings, His miracles, and the authority with which He spoke. The Pharisees, a group of religious leaders known for their strict interpretation of the law of Moses, took notice that Jesus was gaining many disciples. Crowds were turning away from the old systems that measured righteousness by rules and reputation to follow Him. Rather than remain in Judea and intensify the tension, Jesus left and began His journey toward Galilee (John 4:1–3).

Weary from His journey, Jesus stopped to rest at a well in Sychar. But it wasn't only physical exhaustion that brought Him there. What seemed like an ordinary stop was actually part of God's plan, filled with purpose and intention.

Most Jews traveling that route would take the longer way around Samaria to avoid contact with the Samaritan people. The tension between Jews and Samaritans had lasted for centuries, rooted in opposing claims over true worship and contested ancestry. Both groups traced their lineage back to Jacob, yet they were sharply opposed. The Samaritans, descendants of Israelites who had intermarried with foreigners after the Assyrian exile (2 Kings 17:24), built their own temple on Mount Gerizim and worshiped there. In contrast, the Jews worshiped in

Jerusalem. The Samaritans' worship was a blend of devotion to God (Yahweh) and elements of pagan practices (2 Kings 17:33). The two groups disagreed on what true worship looked like and where it should take place. For many Jews, Samaria was a place to avoid, but Jesus chose to pass straight through it, a decision that was uncommon but clearly intentional.

When Jesus reached the outskirts of the Samaritan town of Sychar, located near the plot of land Jacob gave to his son Joseph (John 4:5; Genesis 33:18–19), He stopped at a well that held deep significance. This was Jacob's well, a shared landmark with both historical and spiritual meaning. It was here that Jesus chose to rest during His journey.

While resting, a Samaritan woman approached the well with her water jar. Most women came to the well early in the morning or late in the evening when the air was cool and crowds gathered. But she came at noon, likely to avoid the stares and judgments that followed her. Scripture later reveals that she had been married five times and was now living with a man who was not her husband (John 4:18).

When she approached the well, Jesus spoke first: "Will you give Me a drink?" (John 4:7). She was startled because Jews and Samaritans didn't speak to one another, let alone ask for a drink. Yet here was Jesus, breaking centuries of tension with one simple question, opening the door to a moment that would change her life.

Day 1: The Intersection of Need and Grace

"Jesus knew the Pharisees heard that he was baptizing and making more disciples than John (though Jesus himself didn't baptize them; his disciples did). So, he left Judea and returned to Galilee. He had to go through Samaria on the way. Eventually, he came to the Samaritan village of Sychar, near the field that Jacob gave to his son Joseph. Jacob's well was there; and Jesus, tired from the long walk, sat wearily beside the well about noontime" - John 4:1–6, NLT

At first glance, it may seem like Scripture is simply recording Jesus' travel route from one region to another, but beneath what seems like a simple geographical note is a subtle glimpse into the heart of God. By this point in Jesus' ministry, His influence was growing rapidly, and the Pharisees began to pay close attention to His impact across the region. As mentioned in the overview, the tension between the Jews and Samaritans ran deep. The Pharisees were respected for their knowledge and discipline, but their obsession with external obedience often blinded them to the deeper work God longed to do within. Their religion was meticulous but lacked mercy, and their desire to appear righteous became performance rather than obedience.

But Jesus' message threatened and exposed their pretense. He offered what rules and human effort never could, a way back to the Father's heart that went deeper than religious rituals. His words awakened hearts, and His presence alone carried life. People began to leave systems that had burdened them for years because they found something in Jesus they had never known before: compassion and grace that disrupted self-righteousness and outward performances.

When word reached the Pharisees about how many were turning toward Jesus, He left Judea and began His journey to Galilee. Rather than taking the longer route *around* Samaria, as many Jews did to avoid it, He took the shorter path straight through. It might have seemed like a convenient change in direction, but Scripture makes it clear that His path was intentional. It says He *had* to go through Samaria. Not out of convenience or efficiency, but because He *had* to. The New King James Version says, "He *needed* to go through Samaria."

Those words carry weight because no faithful Jew had to, or needed to, go through Samaria. Avoidance had long been the accepted practice, shaped by generations of division. What began as disagreements over worship and lineage eventually hardened into distance and resentment between the two.

So why did Jesus have to go that way? Not because there wasn't another road, but because love and compassion guided His steps. He wasn't following the path of convenience but one of purpose. There was a story of redemption unfolding beneath the surface of His journey, one that would lead Him right to a woman who had been carrying the weight of rejection, isolation, and misunderstanding.

When Jesus reached Sychar, He stopped at Jacob's well. The Scripture says it was about noon, and He was tired from the journey. He sat there waiting for this woman whose life He was about to redirect before she ever knew He was waiting for her. That is what His grace looks like. Deliberate and purposeful. He moves toward the places others overlook and positions Himself where the unseen and forgotten are.

Before the woman ever arrived at the well, grace was already there, reminding us that God often puts what we need in place long before we know what to ask for (Matthew 6:8; Romans 8:26, NLT).

He *had* to go through Samaria because the love of God doesn't avoid us or take detours. It crosses the boundaries shaped by history, gender, ethnicity, religion, and denominations, reaching for the heart that needs Him. His stop in Sychar held purpose by marking the place where grace would soon intersect with need.

Reflection: Jesus didn't move according to what was customary or permitted. He moved toward those who others avoided and bypassed. Before the Samaritan woman arrived at the well, Jesus was already there, positioned where grace and mercy would soon confront exclusion, isolation, and shame. Let this assurance strengthen your faith and shape how you wait on God for what you need.

Prayer: Father, thank You for being a God who pursues with intention and love. I ask that You help me recognize

Your pursuit of me and trust that You know what I need before I even ask. Teach me to trust Your timing, not mine. Thank You for Your grace that reaches further than I deserve. In Jesus' name, Amen.

Day 2: Breaking Barriers

"Soon a Samaritan woman came to draw water, and Jesus said to her, "Please give me a drink." He was alone at the time because His disciples had gone into the village to buy some food." - John 4:7–8, NLT

The Samaritan woman arrived at the well and found Jesus already sitting there. Drawing water was something she did regularly, but she also had specific reasons for coming at noon. Women typically avoided the well at that hour because it was the hottest part of the day. They came early in the morning or later in the evening when it was cooler, and usually in a group. The well was a place of community and conversation *(see IVP Bible Background Commentary: New Testament, John 4),* but this woman came at a time when she knew no one else would be there.

It's possible that she chose this time to avoid the comments and assumptions of her community. When a person's life is marked by a compromised reputation, isolation can feel safer than facing the judgments of others. She came to draw water and move on, unaware that God would bring her face to face with Jesus, who would speak to the areas of her life shaped by shame and ridicule. She wasn't just carrying a water jar; she was carrying the weight of rejection and the exhaustion of constantly starting over. Yet, the hour she attempted to avoid people became the hour she encountered Jesus.

Jesus initiated the conversation by asking, "Will you give Me a drink?" (John 4:7). He didn't start with correction or exposure but with vulnerability. The Source of life, the One who created water, expressed a need by asking for a drink. The Creator sat beside His creation and met her in something routine, showing that no moment is too small for His presence and grace. Before revealing who He was, He treated her with the dignity that others had denied her by simply starting a conversation with her.

It sounds simple, but it broke every social and cultural rule of that time. A Jewish man speaking to a Samaritan woman alone was unheard of, but Jesus didn't hesitate to engage her. He began the conversation by requesting water, which would soon reveal a deeper thirst in her.

"You are a Jew, and I am a Samaritan woman. Why are you asking me for a drink?" (John 4:9). Her response reflects the social reality she lived in. As a Samaritan and a woman, she understood the boundaries that defined interactions like this and responded accordingly. Her words pointed to a lifetime of barriers shaped by a society where both her ethnicity and gender worked against her.

But that was exactly why Jesus was there. He doesn't move according to what should or shouldn't be done. He steps into spaces others avoid and crosses through walls built by pride and prejudice. He starts the conversations no one else dares to begin because His love doesn't avoid what breaks us.

This encounter at the well is more than history. It's a picture of how Jesus approaches us today. He meets us right in our wounded places and speaks with grace, truth, and a love that reaches beyond our defenses.

It's possible that this is what He's doing in your story right now. The places marked by letdowns or heartbreak might be exactly where He's waiting to meet you. He's not distant from your present struggles, and He's not put off by your past. He's fully engaged in our affairs and invites us into rest and freedom that only He can give.

The woman thought she was coming to draw water, but Heaven arranged an encounter. The time she chose to avoid others became the very moment and place she encountered the Savior who would change her life. The routines of daily life can be the very places where Jesus steps into the ordinary and makes Himself known. He can take what feels common and turn it into a meeting place for redemption.

Reflection: Jesus met the Samaritan woman at a time she likely hoped to remain unseen, and He does the same with us. There's no boundary He hesitates to cross and no moment too ordinary for His presence. God is present and intentional even in what we consider routine. Make room for moments where you intentionally receive connection with God instead of expecting distance.

Prayer: Father, thank You for meeting me in the places I shrink away from and for crossing the walls I build. Help me recognize Your nearness where I expect distance. Lead me out of avoidance and into freedom, and reassure me that nothing about me is too complicated for Your grace. In Jesus' name, Amen.

Day 3: If You Knew the Gift of God

"The woman was surprised, for Jews refuse to have anything to do with Samaritans. She said to Jesus, "You are a Jew, and I am a Samaritan woman. Why are you asking me for a drink?" Jesus replied, "If you only knew the gift God has for you and who you are speaking to, you would ask me, and I would give you living water." - John 4:9-10, NLT

By the time Jesus begins to speak of living water, the moment transitions into something the woman didn't anticipate. What started as a simple request for water opens an invitation to her that reaches beyond an immediate, surface-level need.

In that moment, the well becomes more than a place to draw water; it becomes a reflection of the life she has been living. She came to the well for water, but Jesus speaks to what keeps bringing her back. She returns again and again to the same place, drawing from the same source, carrying burdens she learned to live with rather than confront. Jesus sees what's gone unaddressed and speaks directly to it. The woman who tried to stay unseen is now face to face with the One she can't hide from.

At first, His request catches her off guard. Her circumstances taught her what to expect from people, so caution and defense rise almost instinctively. "You are a Jew, and I am a Samaritan woman. Why are you asking me for a drink?" Her words point to the cultural and religious boundaries that shaped her entire life, but they also show her trying to understand why He crossed boundaries others never would.

Jesus doesn't step back or challenge her hesitation. His response to her moves past her resistance to the need she doesn't have words for. "If you knew the gift of God, and who is asking you for a drink, you would have asked Him, and He would have given you living water."

Those words marked a turning point for her. "If you knew…"

He wasn't giving her more knowledge or rules to follow; He was inviting her to see beyond the limits of what she had always known. Jesus bypassed her physical need for water and revealed the deeper thirst she had been carrying. He was inviting her to exchange what was temporary for what was eternal.

This moment wasn't about tradition or religion. It was about a tired soul meeting the only One who could renew it. Jesus wasn't offering her a new method, a spiritual checklist, ideas to adopt, or habits to refine. He was revealing Himself as the One her heart was yearning for beneath every attempt to cope.

When we're drowning in thoughts and emotions we're unable to make sense of, we often reach for what's familiar as a way to stay afloat. For some, that looks like hoping a relationship will ease the fear of being alone, or cover wounds that haven't been addressed. For others, it's a career expected to provide a sense of worth or capability. Sometimes, it's marriage, assumed to fix what existed long before the wedding day, or titles used to hide parts of ourselves we don't want seen. Routines, distractions, and relationships can relieve us momentarily, but they don't address the root of the matter.

The problem isn't desiring marriage, love, or a meaningful career. The danger comes when we expect them to bear the weight of rebuilding identity, or healing deep wounds. Eventually, they reveal their limits, reminding us they were never meant to do what only God can do.

The well in her story wasn't just a location; Jesus used it to represent the places and things we keep drawing from, even though they fall short of what our heart truly needs. And it's often in those very places that Jesus shifts our focus toward what actually brings life. He speaks to us the same words He spoke to her: "If you knew the gift of God."

If you knew how deep His love runs, how wide His grace reaches, and how patient His mercy is, you would stop reaching for what fades and start resting in what eternalizes. Because when you begin to see the gift for what it truly is, unearned, undeserved, and freely given, you'll begin to realize grace and salvation could never come from your efforts or the pursuits of life. He moves beyond what we think we want and reveals what we truly need, not to embarass us, but to heal and fill us with what satisfies and sustains.

He still speaks those words today, "If you knew the gift of God."

Reflection: Jesus used the well to mirror a deeper pattern in the Samaritan woman's life, showing her that what she kept returning to couldn't quench the real thirst inside her. He redirected her focus to the Gift right in front of her, the One who could satisfy what nothing else could. He still meets us this way, shifting our attention from what's temporary to what's truly life-giving. His grace reveals that nothing we've depended on compares to what He freely gives.

Invite God to show you what you've been reaching for apart from Him, and ask Him to redirect your heart toward what truly brings life.

Prayer: Father, show me where I have been reaching for what cannot satisfy, and help me receive what only You can give. Help me recognize the needs driving my habits, and turn to You with an open heart. Teach me to receive Your grace as the gift that it is and to rest in the living water You freely provide. Draw me closer to what truly brings life. In Jesus' name, Amen.

Day 4: The Source That Never Runs Dry

"But sir, you don't have a rope or a bucket," she said, "and this well is very deep. Where would you get this living water? And besides, do you think you're greater than our ancestor Jacob, who gave us this well? How can you offer better water than he and his sons and his animals enjoyed?" Jesus replied, "Anyone who drinks this water will soon become thirsty again. But those who drink the water I give will never be thirsty again. It becomes a fresh, bubbling spring within them, giving them eternal life." - John 4:11–14, NLT

When Jesus spoke of living water, the Samaritan woman responded from the only perspective she knew, one shaped by survival and the routine of returning to the well. She wasn't openly rejecting Him, but she was pushing back by reasoning through what felt logical to her. Many of us respond the same way when God speaks beyond what we can immediately understand. She heard His words but processed them through her lived experiences. She looked at the well and said, "You have nothing to draw with, and the well is deep." In her mind, the depth of the well became the reason Jesus' offer wasn't possible.

How often do we do the same thing? We look at our circumstances and immediately tell God how deep it is, how hard it is, or how impossible it seems. We don't always say these things out loud, but they surface in our thoughts: Lord, how are You going to help me through this? Can You really reach me in what feels like a pit? This feels too deep, too tangled, too far gone. I don't see a way out, so how could You possibly help me? We measure what's possible through Him by our own limitations, and forget that He is limitless and not subject to those same restraints.

Her eyes were fixed on what was visible: the depth of the well and the fact that Jesus had no bucket. She couldn't understand how this Man could offer water when He had nothing to draw it with. But what He was offering wasn't something that could be physically accessed. The One speaking to her held within Himself a source of living water that never runs dry.

Whether you've grown up in the faith or are new to it altogether, it's easy to look at your own "well" and only see the depth of the problem. Just like the Samaritan woman, we start to question whether God can reach into the places that feel beyond repair. We look at what seems impossible and measure His power by what we can understand. But Living Water is not drawn with a bucket and is not confined to systems or steps. Jesus speaks a word, and life comes forth.

Then the woman asks, "Are You greater than our father Jacob?" Her question revealed that her trust still lay in what had been familiar to her. Jacob's well represented more than water; it symbolized identity and legacy. To her, Jacob was the one who secured what generations depended on. But in exalting the gift, she did not recognize that she was face to face with the Giver

Himself. She still couldn't see that the One standing before her was greater than the one who dug the well.

How often have we done the same? We cling to systems, structures, and people because they're familiar, even when they no longer foster growth. Throughout the Old Testament, God used laws, rituals, and patterns to show what the law could not accomplish and directed us toward Christ, who alone fulfills it. Scripture addresses this in Colossians 2:16–17 (NKJV): "So let no one judge you in food or in drink, or regarding a festival or a new moon or sabbaths, which are a shadow of things to come, but the substance is of Christ." What once guided us was always meant to lead us to Christ, not take His place. Until we let Him be enough, we will keep turning to broken cisterns that cannot sustain life, rather than receiving the fullness found in Christ.

Jesus continues and says, "Anyone who drinks this water will be thirsty again." His words cut through every illusion that anything temporary can truly sustain us. Every earthly well, no matter how deep or dependable, eventually runs dry. It may offer temporary relief or pleasure, but it cannot sustain you. Relationships, success, and recognition are not wrong to desire, but they were never meant to replace the One who restores us from within. We can reach the goal, achieve the milestone, find the thing we thought would complete us, and still feel parched.

God is not offering you another method of survival but an entirely new life. The water He gives does not come from the earth; it flows from His very being. It is His Spirit working within, restoring, cleansing, healing, and transforming you. It reminds me of the same current the prophet Ezekiel saw flowing from the temple, bringing life wherever it went (Ezekiel 47). Everything the river touched began to live again. That vision was a glimpse of what Jesus now offers: the indwelling Spirit that revives what is barren, strengthens what is weak, and turns emptiness into fruitfulness.

This is not a promise of ease but of fullness. Jesus never promised that we would be spared from pain or disappointment. In fact, He told His disciples, "Here on earth you will have many trials and sorrows. But take heart, because I have overcome the world" (John 16:33 NLT). And He also said, "My purpose is to give them a rich and satisfying life" (John 10:10 NLT). What He offers isn't shaken by seasons or circumstances. It sustains when strength fails and keeps us going when hope feels distant.

That is the difference between lowering your bucket into a well that empties and drawing from the fountain of living water that never runs dry. One depends on what we can draw for ourselves; the other depends on the One who supplies us. The woman came with her jar, expecting to fill it and return the next day. But Jesus offered something that would impart new life within her.

When we drink from this Living Water, our striving gives way to rest. The need to prove ourselves, to be seen, and validated by others begins to lose its grip. The same Spirit that met her that day still fills hearts today, not to make us momentarily content, but to gird us in the truth that what we have in Him is complete. His love doesn't patch the cracks; it builds something completely new.

Where love was conditional, He loves without measure. Where life stripped more than it gave, He restores what was fractured and makes all things new.

Reflect: The woman heard Jesus speak of living water and immediately measured His words against what she could see. The well was deep, He had no bucket, and in her mind, that meant His offer was unrealistic. We often do the same when we assume God is limited by what feels impossible to us. But His work in our lives is not restricted to our resources, our understanding, or our circumstances. The living water He gives moves beyond what we can reason with and meets needs we cannot reach by our own efforts.

In what ways have you been using your own logic as the metric for deciding what God can or cannot do?

Prayer: Father, thank You for offering what no earthly source can give. Help me recognize the places where I keep returning to what cannot satisfy, and teach me to turn toward You instead. Fill the empty places within me with the life, peace, and renewal that only Your Spirit provides. Anchor my heart in the truth that You are the source that never runs dry. In Jesus' name, Amen.

Day 5: Exposing Patterns

"Please, sir," the woman said, "give me this water! Then I'll never be thirsty again, and I won't have to come here to get water." "Go and get your husband," Jesus told her. "I don't have a husband," the woman replied. Jesus said, "You're right! You don't have a husband, for you have had five husbands, and you aren't even married to the man you're living with now. You certainly spoke the truth!" - John 4:15–18, NLT

What sounds like a simple request is actually the cry of a desperate heart: "Sir, give me this water so that I'll never be thirsty again, and have to keep coming here to draw water" (John 4:15).

She doesn't even realize the weight of what she's asking for. Her heart is open to His offer, but her perspective is still limited to what the eye can see. When she hears Jesus talking about water, she's thinking of relief from her daily walk to the well and the tiring routine she repeats every single day. To her, His offer sounds like a convenient option. She's focused on what would help her physically, unaware that Jesus is reaching for her wounded soul.

He wasn't offering to remove her daily responsibilities or provide an escape from them. He was addressing something beneath the surface of her life. When she says, "Give me this water," she is hoping for rest from the daily strain, but He wants to give her rest in her soul. She's thinking about quenching her body's thirst, but He is addressing her soul's thirst.

Then He says, "Go, call your husband and come back" (v. 16). Notice that as soon as she asks for the living water, Jesus brings up her husband. At first, His words seem unrelated and even abrupt, but that timing matters. Before God can pour new life into a vessel, He first makes room for it. Jesus taught that new wine cannot be poured into old wineskins without causing them to burst. The old container cannot hold what is new (Matthew 9:17, Mark 2:22, Luke 5:37–38, NLT). In the same way, what God offers cannot take root in a heart that is still crowded. Living water flows where truth has been welcomed, and where what we keep returning to is uprooted.

The woman then replies, "I have no husband" (v. 17). With those few words, she steps into the truth about her life with no excuses. Just honesty before the One who already knows, and that honesty became the doorway to her healing.

Jesus responds, "You are right when you say you have no husband. The fact is, you have had five husbands, and the man you now have is not your husband. What you have said is quite true" (v. 18). Notice His words don't condemn her; they confront the truth about her life.

Scripture doesn't tell us why she had been married five times. In a patriarchal society, women often needed male provision in order to survive. It's entirely possible that she was repeatedly put away rather than choosing to leave, and it's also possible she was widowed a few times. Those details aren't included in the scriptures. What the text makes clear is not the cause of her failed marriages, but the pattern and significance of them. Jesus deemed her relational history worth bringing to the surface to reveal what had been shaping her life. What Jesus uncovers is the search to fill a void through people and cycles. For her, it was men, one after another, each representing unaddressed, wounded roots that continued to resurface.

If we're honest, that same cycle may exist in many of us. It may not look like five husbands, but it carries the same desire to feel validated, whole, and securely loved. Sometimes it shows up as busyness, keeping us from facing what feels empty inside. Sometimes it looks like shrinking ourselves to keep the peace, clinging to approval, or chasing new beginnings whenever being still feels uncomfortable. We know what it's like to hope this time will be different and still fall back into the same old patterns. We gravitate toward what's familiar, even when it keeps leading us to the same outcome.

Emptiness, discouragement, insecurity, fear, shame and disappointment were never meant to be accepted or managed; they serve as a reminder of our need for Jesus. He reveals the chains so He can remove them. He exposes what we hide, not to humiliate us, but to set us free. That's the sound of grace, not judgment. Judgment assigns blame, and grace assigns a way forward. He invites us to see both the wound and the impact, and to acknowledge the truth without being condemned by it. And once we do, we recognize He extends grace right in the very places we thought disqualified us.

Every failed attempt to be loved and every search for belonging may have led us to places marked by disappointment and regret, but even there, His mercy finds us. The Lord is "close to the brokenhearted and rescues those whose spirits are crushed," (Psalm 34:18) not as an observer, but as a restorer. That nearness was what the Samaritan woman felt as He spoke: a love that did not turn away or condemn but began to heal her.

You may not be hiding behind a well, but you know what it feels like to hide behind a smile or composure. You show up, serve, and care for everyone else, even when your own heart is tired. You move through days holding it together, masking the hurt with productivity and staying strong because you've learned there's no room for brokenness. As if acknowledging it would somehow mean you lack faith. But deep down, there's an exhaustion from always having to be okay. You've built walls to protect yourself, and healing has felt out of reach because of them. But Jesus is not put off by your defenses. He pursues you the way He pursued the woman at the well and the way He described the Good Shepherd who goes after the one lost sheep until He finds it (Luke 15:4).

God desires truth in the innermost being (Psalm 51:6). He cannot heal what we continue to avoid. But when we bring Him our unfiltered, raw, and unedited honesty, grace floods in like water through stone. The well of shame begins to close, and the well of life begins to flow.

The Samaritan woman came to the well to draw water with a bucket, but she became the vessel. And so can we, when we receive what He offers, Living Water for the weary soul.

Reflection: When Jesus told the Samaritan woman to bring her husband, He wasn't exposing her to embarrass her. He was revealing what she'd spent years avoiding rather than confronting. In that moment, He showed her that real transformation begins when we stop trying to compensate for what's broken and allow the truth to set us free.

Prayer: Father, thank You for speaking to the parts of me I try to hide. Help me recognize the patterns that drain me and face them with honesty before You. Thank You that Your truth always comes with grace and that You bring to light what You intend to heal. Fill the empty places within me and restore what has been worn thin. In Jesus' name, Amen.

Day 6 - More Than Just A Man

"The woman said to Him, 'Sir, I perceive that You are a prophet." - John 4:19, NKJV

When the Samaritan woman said, "Sir, I perceive that You are a prophet," she wasn't responding emotionally or impulsively. She realized this Man knew intimate details of her life, though He never met her. Jesus spoke with insight, certainty, and accuracy. In that moment, He was no longer just a man sitting by a well with no bucket, He was someone speaking with authority that exceeded human explanation. The subject of the conversation didn't change, but her understanding of Who was addressing her began to.

Scripture consistently shows that acknowledgment of who He is shapes what follows in our lives. When Isaiah saw the Lord "high and lifted up" (Isaiah 6:1, NLT), his recognition led to his confession: "I am doomed, for I am a sinful man" (Isaiah 6:5). God then removed his guilt and atoned for his sin (Isaiah 6:6–7). Only after this did Isaiah respond to God's call, "Here am I. Send me!" (Isaiah 6:8).

The same pattern appears in the Apostle Paul's conversion on the road to Damascus. What changed his life was not human effort or a change in behavior, but the moment he realized who Jesus was. He was confronted with the identity of the One he was opposing. When he asked, "Who are You, Lord?" and heard the answer, "I am Jesus, the one you are persecuting" (Acts 9:5, NLT), everything that followed flowed from that acknowledgment.

John 9 reflects this same progression. The man born blind receives physical sight by Jesus early in the chapter, but his understanding of who Jesus is develops over time. He first refers to Him as "the man they call Jesus" (v. 11), then says, "He must be a prophet" (v. 17). When questioned by the Pharisees, he testifies, "I was blind, and now I can see!" (v. 25). Later, after Jesus reveals Himself as the Son of Man (v. 35–37), the man responds, "Yes, Lord, I believe" and he worships Him (v. 38). His worship flowed from a clarified understanding of who Jesus was. That is what was *beginning* to happen at the well. The Samaritan woman's recognition of Christ's sovereignty had begun, though not yet complete.

Ask yourself: How are you perceiving Him right now? As distant? Silent? A historical figure? Or as the sovereign One who knows and loves you? We begin to recognize God rightly when we stop filtering Him through our experiences and allow His Word to reveal who He is.

As the Samaritan woman began to recognize who He was, she understood that this was no ordinary encounter. She was not speaking with someone limited by human knowledge, but with One who saw beyond the surface. She realized this was more than an ordinary man.

Reflection: The Samaritan woman realized the One before her saw her and spoke with an authority that uncovered her life. Until Jesus is seen as more than a historical figure or just a man that once walked the earth, He will be approached casually, heard selectively, and responded to on our own terms.

Prayer: Father, open my eyes to see You clearly. Remove the assumptions, fears, and past experiences that have shaped how I perceive You. Teach me to recognize Your presence in ways I may have overlooked and anchor my heart in the truth of who You are. Let clarity replace confusion and trust replace hesitation as You reshape the way I see you. In Jesus' name, Amen.

Chapter 7: Worship in Spirit and Truth

"So tell me, why is it that you Jews insist that Jerusalem is the only place of worship, while we Samaritans claim it is here at Mount Gerizim, where our ancestors worshiped?" Jesus replied, "Believe me, dear woman, the time is coming when it will no longer matter whether you worship the Father on this mountain or in Jerusalem. You Samaritans know very little about the one you worship, while we Jews know all about him, for salvation comes through the Jews. But the time is coming, indeed it is here now, when true worshipers will worship the Father in spirit and in truth. The Father is looking for those who will worship him that way. For God is Spirit, so those who worship him must worship in spirit and in truth" - John 4:20–24, NLT

After recognizing Jesuus as a prophet (v.19), the Samaritan woman turned to a question she believed He could answer: where worship should take place.

Her understanding of worship had been shaped by culture and tradition. When she referred to the mountain, she was asking which place of worship was recognized as legitimate. But Jesus shifted her focus beyond location and tradition and redirected her from what's seen to what's unseen. He tells her that the hour has come when worship will no longer be defined by temples, mountains, or rituals, but by the posture of the heart. In just one conversation, He dismantles every structure built around performance and points to what the Father truly seeks: those who will worship Him in spirit and in truth.

To worship in Spirit means to rely completely on the work of God within us rather than on our own strength. Paul describes it this way: "For we who worship by the Spirit of God are the ones who are truly circumcised. We rely on what Christ Jesus has done for us. We put no confidence in human effort" (Philippians 3:3, NLT). This is not to say that our worship should never be expressed outwardly, but that our confidence must rest in what Christ has accomplished, not in how we perform. True worship flows from hearts made alive by grace, and hearts that depend on His Spirit to lead and shape their response. It is the surrender of self-effort and the yielding of every part of us to the God who loves us beyond measure.

To worship in truth means more than honesty; it means living in a sound awareness of who God is and responding to Him as He truly deserves. Jesus said, "Your word is truth" (John 17:17), showing that truth is not emotion but reality revealed through His Word. Real worship begins when our hearts yield to that reality, and when what we believe starts to shape how we live. The psalmist writes, "The Lord is close to all who call on him, yes, to all who call on him in truth" (Psalm 145:18 NLT). God draws near to the one who comes with sincerity, who is done performing and simply chooses to stand before Him without pretense.

When Jesus says, "The Father is looking," He's showing us something almost hard to grasp. God seeks. The same Creator who spoke worlds into being is searching, not for performance or grand sacrifices, but for hearts that are loyal, genuine, and willing to love Him back. Scripture says His eyes move throughout the earth, looking for those whose hearts are fully devoted to Him (2 Chronicles 16:9). That's what moves Him. Not performance, just desperation that lives in the heart of someone who desires Him. The same God who needs nothing chooses to draw near to those who worship in spirit and in truth.

So, it's not about preference, a stage, or a place. Every space becomes an altar when our hearts turn toward Him. The kitchen, the commute, wherever you stand, sit, break down, gather with others, or kneel, that's where worship can arise. Not because the setting holds the power, but because God does. Not because of the room you're in, but because God is in the room. Not because a space is prepared a certain way, but because your heart is. Not because of a location, but because He is omnipresent and fills every space that exists.

The woman had been taught that worship was something to be performed through priests and rituals. But Jesus sat beside her and offered her direct access to the presence of God. The barriers of gender, culture, and history still existed in the world, but in that moment, Jesus moved beyond them. The Samaritan woman was being invited into a worship that could not be contained by walls or divided by heritage.

Every heart will worship something because worship is embedded in our design. The question is not *if* we worship, but *what* or *who* we worship. Some bow to success, others to control, pride, comfort, affirmation, or relational security. But only worship directed toward the living God brings freedom. Everything else eventually demands and costs more than it gives.

You may have learned to worship through expressions that were passed down to you or have been taught what it's supposed to look like. Maybe you were told that your closeness to God depended on how much you did, or how closely you followed a certain tradition or culture. But Jesus dismantles that illusion by showing that the Father's gaze reaches beyond outward motion and looks for what cannot be performed: a heart turned honestly toward Him.

This is not a dismissal of cultural or outward expressions of worship. Such expressions can be meaningful and beautiful when they arise from the heart and remain rooted in the truth of who God is. But they are just that: expressions of worship, not the foundation or proof of it. When you worship in spirit and truth, it extends beyond moments and expressions and becomes how you live.

"So dear brothers and sisters, I plead with you to give your bodies to God because of all he has done for you. Let them be a living and holy sacrifice, the kind he will find acceptable. This is truly the way to worship him." Romans 12:1 (NLT)

Reflection: When the Samaritan woman spoke about where worship was supposed to happen, she was expressing what she had been taught. By referencing the mountain, she was revealing the system that she believed legitimate worship was. But Jesus drew the conversation out of geography and into the heart. Worship was no longer bound to a location or a culture but redefined as a response to God's sovereignty. When worship moves from performance to connection, it stops being something we try to achieve and becomes the natural expression of a heart aligned with Him.

Have you confined your worship to certain places, moods, or moments? How might your relationship with God deepen if you learned to worship Him beyond those limitations?

Prayer: Father, teach me to worship You with a heart aligned to truth and guided by Your Spirit. Remove the habits, assumptions, and limitations that have shaped how I approach You. Let my worship flow from sincerity rather than routine, and from awareness rather than performance. Draw my heart into deeper reverence and genuine connection with You. In Jesus' name, Amen.

Day 8: The Messiah Revealed

"The woman said, 'I know the Messiah is coming, the one who is called Christ. When he comes, he will explain everything to us.' Then Jesus told her, 'I am the Messiah!" - John 4:25–26, NLT

The word *Messiah* comes from the Hebrew *Mashiach*, meaning "the Anointed One." In Greek, it is *Christos*, the title we know as *Christ.* In Scripture, anointing signifies being set apart and commissioned by God for a specific purpose. Jesus is the Anointed One, set apart to bear sin, restore what was lost, and reign in righteousness.

When the Samaritan woman spoke of the Messiah, she was expressing a hope carried through generations and repeating what she had been taught all her life. It was a standard belief among the Samaritans that the Messiah would one day come. Her understanding of who she was speaking to was still growing. She knew this was no ordinary man, but she did not yet know He was the Messiah. Then Jesus revealed, "I am the Messiah."

In that moment, the hope of nations stood before her, fulfilling what the prophets had long spoken of. For the first time, Jesus revealed His identity not to a ruler or a priest, but to an outcast woman who only understood part of the story. He revealed Himself as the long-awaited Messiah to a woman others dismissed, showing that He's not governed by social rank or gender.

Jesus stepped into a moment marked by exclusion and turned it into a place of redemption. The same God who said, "I will make you a light to the Gentiles, and you will bring my salvation to the ends of the earth" (Isaiah 49:6) was fulfilling that promise in an ordinary moment at a well in Sychar. Not on a grand stage, not before an audience, not through religious authority, but to a woman whose life choices disqualified her in the eyes of many.

The Samaritan woman did not have it all figured out, but she continued engaging Jesus with an open heart. That was the moment the long-awaited Messiah made Himself known. God honors openness, not having all the answers.

When Jesus reveals Himself, everything in you reorients. You may still have questions, but you no longer question who holds the answer. What was once distant became personal, and that moment redirected her life. That truth remains today. Recognizing Him for who He is shifts us from chasing short-lived relief to leaning into the life-giving Spirit.

Reflection: The Samaritan woman expected the Messiah to arrive someday, somewhere else, through someone more qualified than her. Yet Jesus chose that moment at the well to reveal who He was. Her limited understanding didn't disqualify her from receiving a revelation meant to change her life. It reminds us that God often makes Himself known in places we never thought to look and in moments we assumed were ordinary. When He reveals

Himself, certainty replaces confusion, and faith rises where hesitation once lived.

Have you ever assumed God would reveal Himself somewhere else or to someone else, and not in your own life?

Prayer: Father, help me recognize who You are through Your Word and through the ways You are already at work in my life. Set my heart in a place where I can respond to the truth, even when I don't fully understand everything. Remove the assumptions that have shaped my view of You and give me a grounded awareness of Your goodness. Let the reality of who You are become clearer and more rooted in me. In Jesus' name, Amen.

Day 9: She Left Her Jar

"Just then his disciples came back. They were shocked to find him talking to a woman, but none of them had the nerve to ask, 'What do you want with her?' or 'Why are you talking to her?' The woman left her water jar beside the well and ran back to the village, telling everyone, 'Come and see a man who told me everything I ever did! Could he possibly be the Messiah?" - John 4:27–29, NLT

The disciples were caught off guard seeing Jesus speaking with the Samaritan woman. Everything about this moment went against what they were accustomed to. But Jesus didn't move according to the cultural lines or religious boundaries of that time. He moved toward the very person others avoided.

Then Scripture adds a small but important detail: "The woman left her water jar." That jar may have been for water, but it also mirrored how she had been living. Every trip to that well reflected the attempt to meet her own need in her own strength. It was the cycle of survival: drawing, filling, emptying, and returning. It's a picture of what it's like to live, trying to fill a void that only God can.

That moment at the well became more than a daily routine; it became an altar of exchange. She didn't just walk away from an object; she walked away from a pattern. That jar she left behind symbolized the systems and cycles she relied on to manage her brokeness instead of bringing it to God.

Many of us have stood at our own wells, praying for change while gripping what needs to be released. We cry, we confess, we respond to altar calls, but we walk away holding the same jar, the same patterns, the same habits, the same attachments that keep us bound. We come before God with sincerity, asking Him to do something new, while our hands remain wrapped around what is familiar. We ask for breakthrough while clinging to what breaks us. We pray for freedom while carrying the very things that keep us bound. And just like the woman at the well, we keep returning to places that cannot sustain us, hoping they will fill what they never could.

For some, that "jar" looks like:

The relationship that drains more than it supports your growth: I know it's tempting to text back, to call back, to respond, or to go back to the person causing you harm. It's tempting to try again, believing this time will be different, but you already know it won't give you anything different from the last time. You've been down this road before. You've hoped, you've tried, you've convinced yourself that trying one more time will work, but it never does. It leaves you in the same place every time, reaching, waiting, craving, and still coming up hurt and empty.

Overextending yourself: You pour yourself out for everyone but rarely let anyone pour into you. It feels noble, but deep down, it's fueled by fear (and maybe pride) that if you stop giving, you'll stop being valued. The more you live this way, the more you will see that constantly overextending without rest pushes you into a level of burnout you were never meant to live in.

The friendships that no longer align with who you're becoming: You hold on because it feels familiar, but familiarity isn't the same as faithfulness, and it definitely isn't the same as loyalty. Sometimes God asks you to release what's comfortable, not to punish you, but because He's preparing to surround you with people who strengthen what He's building in you. Friendships should support your calling, not suffocate it. And when God leads you away from what no longer aligns with that, letting go can feel like betrayal, but it's making room for what propels you into where He's taking you.

The list goes on, but you get the picture.

Every one of these jars tells the same story: our attempt to manage what only God can heal. And like this woman, we need to decide: will we keep carrying what's familiar, or will we finally lay it down and leave it behind? That well became her altar. Right there, where shame once gripped her, she made an exchange. She let go of what represented her past and embraced who she was in light of that encounter. She didn't say a word, but her leaving that jar spoke volumes.

What happened that day left her with an urgency she didn't have before. She ran back to her village because something within her awakened, and the same woman who used to avoid people now became the one who drew them in. That's what happens when we let go of what weighs us down and make room for what God wants to impart in us.

Scripture says, "Let us strip off every weight that slows us down, especially the sin that so easily trips us up. And let us run with endurance the race God has set before us" (Hebrews 12:1, NLT). Not everything that holds you back is sin; it can also be baggage that hinders you. Some things are simply weights, good things, old things, and familiar things that have outlived their purpose in your life.

When you finally release what's been weighing you down, you'll see why the Samaritan woman didn't hesitate to leave her jar and run like nothing was holding her back.

Reflection: The Samaritan woman's jar represented the life she built around managing brokenness. But after encountering Jesus, she didn't need the same tools to survive. She left behind what belonged to the old version of her. Sometimes the clearest sign of transformation is not what we gain but what we no longer feel the need to carry.

What “jar” have you been carrying that God may be asking you to release? It could be a habit, approval from people, an expectation, a relationship, or mindsets that keep you circling the same place emotionally or spiritually. Bring it before God honestly and take one practical step toward loosening your grip. Freedom begins only when we let go of what’s weighing us down.

Prayer: Father, help me recognize anything I’ve been carrying that no longer belongs in my hands. Give me the courage to release what drains me and the strength to walk away from what keeps me stuck in cycles. Teach me to trust You with what I let go of and to run toward what brings life. Let my surrender create room for Your peace, Your direction, and Your Spirit in me. In Jesus’ name, Amen.

Day 10: "Many Believed Because of Her Testimony"

"Come and see a man who told me everything I ever did! Could he possibly be the Messiah?' So the people came streaming from the village to see him. Many Samaritans from that town believed in him because of the woman's testimony, 'He told me all that I ever did.' When they came out to see him, they begged him to stay in their village. So he stayed for two days, long enough for many more to hear his message and believe. Then they said to the woman, 'Now we believe, not just because of what you told us, but because we have heard him ourselves. Now we know that he is indeed the Savior of the world." - John 4:29, 39–42, NLT

The Samaritan woman didn't keep her encounter with Jesus at the well to herself. The same woman who once avoided her community now ran through the streets, unashamed, proclaiming, "Come and see a man who told me everything I ever did!" One encounter with Jesus moved her from avoidance to boldness, and people came streaming from their homes to see the One she was speaking about. That's what happens when a life truly encounters Jesus, it draws attention not to itself, but to Him.

Her story wasn't scripted or self-centered. She shared what happened to her plainly, and that was enough to draw people toward Jesus.

The essence of a true testimony is not the story itself that changes hearts; it's the God within the story. A testimony is not the Gospel, but it is the evidence, the impact, the fruit, and the living proof of what the Gospel produces in a life. It speaks of a Savior who died, was buried, rose again, and who still redeems and restores today. It doesn't glorify the teller; it glorifies the Redeemer. The Samaritan woman's words drew her neighbors in, but it was Jesus' presence that transformed them. Scripture says, "Many believed because of her testimony, but many more believed when they met Him for themselves."

She didn't point to herself; she pointed to Jesus. That's the power of a redeemed life; it redirects attention from the broken vessel to the One who repairs and fills it. Your testimony carries weight not because of its details, drama, or any "wow" factors, but because it reveals the One who makes all things new.

I remember when I first began sharing my redemption story with others. An elder whom I visited one day said to me, "You know, Nakita, you should keep your story to yourself, between you and God on your knees. People don't need to know your business." The words may have been well-intended, but they circled in my mind for months. However, I knew what God had done in my life was too powerful to stay silent about. The girl who emerged from a place of rejection, relational abuse, fear, addictions, loss, and darkness couldn't help but declare the One who found her there and set her free. John 8:36, NLT says "So if the Son sets you free, you are truly free."

When your story points to Jesus, it becomes a bridge for others to cross into hope. The enemy wants to keep you quiet, but your voice, when surrendered to God, becomes a weapon of mass destruction against the silence and shame that Satan wants you to live in.

Acts 4:20 (NLT): "We cannot stop telling about everything we have seen and heard."

Psalm 107:2 (NLT): "Has the Lord redeemed you? Then speak out! Tell others he has redeemed you from your enemies."

Galatians 6:14 (NLT): "As for me, may I never boast about anything except the cross of our Lord Jesus Christ. Because of that cross, my interest in this world has been crucified, and the world's interest in me has also died."

This is not to suggest that we should share every detail of our lives with everyone. Wisdom and discernment matter. There are times when God will lead you to speak, and times when He will lead you to exercise restraint. But if He prompts you to share, trust that your redemption story has purpose. Someone's faith may begin because of your obedience to speak. If you once walked in darkness and now walk in the light, however that journey unfolded, you have a testimony.

The Samaritan woman's testimony lit a spark, but the fire spread when the people met Jesus themselves. The same is true for you. God doesn't waste your story or discredit you because of it. The parts you thought disqualified you might be the very evidence someone else needs to believe that redemption is possible. Your honesty might be the bridge that leads another person from curiosity or skepticism to faith.

A woman with no social standing, who hid from her community, became the catalyst for an awakening that drew her community to Jesus. That's the power of grace! God used the very thing she once hid as the platform for His glory. The part of her story she most likely wished no one knew became the very proof that God's love reaches where shame lives.

The Samaritans said to the woman, "Now we believe, not just because of what you told us, but because we have heard Him ourselves." You can tell people about Jesus, but they must come to know Him for themselves. That's why the gospel message *cannot* be altered. It doesn't need to be modernized, rebranded, or updated to be relevant. It already carries the power and potency to save. We contend for the faith not by reshaping it to fit the times, but by holding firmly to what's been handed down through the Scriptures and speaking it plainly to the world we're in. He lived, He died, He rose again, and He calls us to repent, believe, and follow Him. That's the message, in that order. The beauty of the Gospel is not in its packaging but in its power to save to the uttermost.

We may not see Jesus face to face on this side of heaven, as the Samaritan woman did, but we have His

Spirit living within us. Jesus said, "It is to your advantage that I go away. For if I do not go away, the Helper will not come to you... But when He, the Spirit of truth, comes, He will guide you into all truth." (John 16:7, 13, NLT). We may not physically walk beside Him, but we walk with the same power that raised Him from the grave (Romans 8:11, NLT), and we hold to the promise that one day we *will* see Him face to face. That is what strengthens us to testify when it would be easier not to.

So be encouraged and know that He who has begun a good work within you, will continue his work until it is finally finished on the day when Christ Jesus returns" (Philippians 1:6, NLT). God saves us by His grace, remains with us through His Spirit, guides us into truth, and sanctifies us along the way. In response, our lives naturally bear witness to who He is and all that He's done.

Reflection: The Samaritan woman's voice carried weight not because she had training, credibility, or came from a lineage of priests, but because something in her had radically changed. Her transformation spoke louder than her history. One honest invitation, "Come and see," opened the door for an entire community to experience Christ for themselves. That is the strength of a life touched by grace. God does not wait for perfection to use us. He works through the surrendered, the willing, and the once broken to draw others toward Him.

Ask God to highlight one person who may need encouragement or hope. Share only what He prompts you to share about His work in your life. Trust that even a small step of obedience can plant a seed that He is able to grow.

Prayer: Father, give me courage to share the parts of my story that reflect Your goodness. Help me speak with humility, sincerity, and wisdom. Use my life as a doorway for others to encounter the hope found in You. Guide my words, and let everything I share point back to Christ. In Jesus' name, Amen.

From my heart to yours,

Thank you for journeying through this devotional book!

Every page, paragraph, and line was prayerfully written with precision, counsel, and with YOU in mind. This book is not meant to be a formula for instant change or a shortcut to healing. It's an invitation to sit with the scriptures, and allow the truth of God's Word to take root and flourish in its own time. I pray this marks the beginning of something new in your life. May you step into a deeper awareness of Christ and the abundant life He offers.

Scripture says, "For we are God's masterpiece. He has created us anew in Christ Jesus, so we can do the good things He planned for us long ago" (Ephesians 2:10, NLT). Walking in that calling requires a willingness to face the wounds God desires to heal. As you respond to the work He wants to do in you, He reveals and restores what sin, fear, and avoidance have fractured, so that your life bears honest witness to His grace and power.

Above all, I pray you walk away holding this close: **God deemed YOU worth saving.** He saw you before you were searching, knew you before you had a physical body, and pursued you before you knew you needed Him. He knows everything about you (Psalm 139, NLT). You are seen, loved, and known by Him, and He'll guide you as you take the next step forward into the liberty and grace He offers through His Son, Jesus.

If you're unsure of what you believe about Jesus, you're invited, in this moment, to turn toward Him and receive the eternal life He offers.

"For this is how God loved the world: He gave his one and only Son, so that everyone who believes in him will not perish but have eternal life."- John 3:16 (NLT)

"And I am certain that God, who began the good work within you, will continue His work until it is finally finished on the day when Christ Jesus returns." - Philippians 1:6 (NLT)

"Search me, O God, and know my heart; test me and know my anxious thoughts. Point out anything in me that offends You, and lead me along the path of everlasting life." - Psalm 139:23–24 (NLT)

"Anyone who belongs to Christ has become a new person. The old life is gone; a new life has begun!" - 2 Corinthians 5:17 (NLT)

Historical & Cultural Notes

2 Kings 17:24–33 – Background on the Assyrian exile and Samaritan ancestry.

Genesis 33:18–19 – Jacob's land near Shechem (Sychar).

IVP Bible Background Commentary: New Testament – Cultural context of wells and public gathering practices.

Colossians 2:16–17 – Shadow and fulfillment theology in Christ.

Ezekiel 47 – Prophetic imagery of life-giving water flowing from the temple.

Scripture Index

Genesis 33:18–19
2 Kings 17:24–33
Isaiah 6:1–8
Ezekiel 47
John 4
John 10:10
John 16:7, 13, 33
Acts 9:5
Colossians 2:16–17
Hebrews 12:1
2 Chronicles 16:9
Psalm 34:18
Psalm 51:6
Psalm 107:2
Psalm 139:23–24
Romans 8:11
Philippians 1:6
2 Corinthians 5:17
Ephesians 2:10
Luke 15:4

Sources & Acknowledgments

The Holy Bible, New Living Translation (NLT). Tyndale House Publishers.

The Holy Bible, New King James Version (NKJV). Thomas Nelson.

Keener, Craig S. The IVP Bible Background Commentary: New Testament. InterVarsity Press.

Edited by: Dr. Elliana Peckings

www.ingramcontent.com/pod-product-compliance
Lightning Source LLC
LaVergne TN
LVHW051021080826
845145LV00009B/2733

* 9 7 8 0 9 9 5 9 3 0 7 4 2 *